MARJORIE WALK

David Phillips

To my wife, Lesley
with much love

INTRODUCTION

Margate cemetery, situated on the outskirts of the town between Saint Gregory's Primary School and Thanet Council's refuse collection site, was founded in 1856 and is a typical Victorian municipal cemetery of some 35 acres. Its rural walks support many mature trees, undisturbed wildlife, and thousands of graves, none of which contain the remains of anybody remotely famous.

Nevertheless, a visit is recommended as many of the gravestones display the superb artistry of the Victorian mason, from an unfurled angel at the head of a modest family grave to the magnificent life-sized Mazeppa stallion atop the tomb of circus showman, John Sanger.

If the visitor enters the cemetery by the pedestrians' entrance and bears right for a few yards, they will encounter the grave of 16 year-old, Marjorie Walk, a local amateur dancer and beauty queen finalist who was killed in the summer of 1938 as the result of an aeroplane crash in the sea off Margate.

Marjorie's death featured prominently in the local newspaper, but the crash also made the front page lead stories in the Daily Mirror, Daily Express, and other nationals. Was this simply because she was young and attractive? A cynic might suggest that in a slow week for news the 5000 holidaymakers on Margate beaches who witnessed the tragedy might have been more likely than not to buy a paper the next day to read about what they'd seen.

Press interest touched on the universal sadness of a young girl's unexpected death, but in just over a year Great Britain would be at war and deaths in the air, at sea and on the ground would become commonplace. Margate cemetery has its own section where war graves are beautifully kept and maintained. Unlike the last resting places of Marjorie Walk and Edmund Betts, her teenage pilot, whose graves have long fallen into neglect.

However a visit to Margate cemetery in spring and summer is hardly a mournful experience. Its rustic beauties and fine memorials will not disappoint, and hopefully, the visitor will stand for a few moments before Marjorie's grave and think of her.

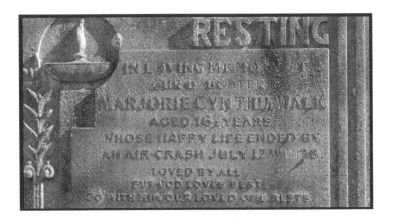

IN LOVING MEMORY OF

OUR DAUGHTER

MARJORIE CYNTHIA WALK

AGED 16½ YEARS

WHOSE HAPPY LIFE ENDED BY

AN AIR-CRASH JULY 17TH 1938.

LOVED BY ALL

BUT GOD LOVES BEST
SO WITH HIM OUR LOVED ONE RESTS

Resting

The word suggests a temporary state,
a periodic repose before resuming
normal movement, a simple pause, hiatus,
recovery of feeling, thought and strength.

Unless the adjective is raised in stone
above a name and date. Another meaning,
the rest conditional: finite with faith,
some future awakening, without faith, endless.

Here at Margate cemetery, confinement
looks a long one — eighty years, eighty
summers since Marjorie (whom God loves best)
was lowered in the ground to start her rest.

Precognition

Did you wake in your sunny bedroom
that Sunday morning and daydream
            about your happy life?

Such a shame you couldn't see
the smiling boy in his aeroplane
            and those icy summer waves.

Sunny Intervals

That Sunday afternoon in Kent:
the temperature was normal for
the time of year, no chance of rain,
a light breeze with sunny intervals.

The air clear, the sea calm,
fine weather for flying aeroplanes,
fine weather for doing something else.

    For anything else.

Sunday For Seven Days

That week in Margate cinemas:
Kay Francis stars in Warners', 'First Lady,
A Radio Murder Mystery';
no swing bands, songs or dancing feet,
would this appeal to Marjorie?

Still less, 'The Last of the Mohicans'
with Wallace Ford — a boys' flick,
long muskets, pistols, bows and arrows,
endless inane conversations,
how could she tap her feet to those?

The pick — if Marjorie had lived —
Sonja Henie and Don Ameche
sing and dance for ninety minutes
uptown at the Astoria,
in Fox's mocking, 'Happy Landing'.

Marjorie Dancing And Singing -1

Those massive Margate fields of browning
corn warming in the July sun,
a morning when she danced alone,
and sang in joy of being young.

She spun, arms stretched towards the sky
and sang that God should give her wings
so she could fly.

High Town

Dances, firework displays, stage shows —
Margate, July, 1938 —
so many amusements to entertain the Joes
and Janes and those who like to stay up late.

Margate by night — a host of ritzy bars,
and even during winter months the flicks
all spoil for choice with first-run Hollywood stars,
epics and quota-quickies thrown in the mix.

Marjorie, so lucky to live here — all
her London friends agree, you never pass
a dull weekend, and life can never pall.
So why bump in the Hawk through Ramsgate grass?

Victorian Architecture

When you skipped down Margate streets,
with an expert buck and wing,
did you see the grand Victorian
houses on either side of you?

Did you like their steep slate roofs
with cosy attic dormers, engraved
cream brackets that ornament the eaves,
octagonal towers like lighthouses?

Did you notice the eyebrow windows,
iconic bays set in patterned brickwork,
ornate carvings on window sills
and interesting date stones?

And if the sky grew dark with rain,
would you keep dry in funny porches
with their complex gingerbread cut-outs
and neo-Georgian spindle work?

Or did you laugh at such pretensions —
saw too well their patent faults,
never dreaming you'd spend forever
among Victorian stones and vaults?

Betty Behenna

A walk-on part in a summer season drama,
best friend of Marjorie, the rising star;
Betty Behenna, the lucky girl who flew
with Edmund Betts and lived to tell the tale.

The girl who waved her best friend off,
then bit her lip and wondered if
she should have said something, then fretted
when the plane did not return.

The girl who fainted when told her friend was lost;
the drive home in the airport car, the staring
from her bedroom window at the sea,
the quandary: how to start her life again.

Dancing With Impatience

'When we got back to the airport, Marjorie
was dancing with impatience.'
    Betty Behenna, Daily Express, 18/7/1938

Marjie grabbed the flying helmet,
leapt into the open cockpit,
Betty had no time to tell her
how the flight had petrified.

Would Marjorie have taken notice?
The boy, the plane, the sea and sky,
the shaking engine, the rush, the leap
of rubber wheels from grass. Like dancing.

Remember When

Remember when
we met the boy
who drove us to
the aerodrome
then wheeled his plane
into the wind
and gunned the engine
into life
and flew you round
the battleship?

I sat and waited
for my turn
picked runway daisies
for a garland
dreamed of Thursday's
competition
crown of Margate
beauty queen
to rule my float
at Carnival.

When you returned
you had no breath
to tell me how
the boy had made
you sick and scared
with crazy stunts

I took your place
gave up my life
to find a fame
in newspapers.

What Does Marjorie Think?

A 'jeau d'esprit', a laugh, a silliness
to go up with a boy she hardly knows,
a novice pilot, hired aircraft, does she
sense the multiplying risks as Edmund
throws the Hawk around the bays of Kent?

Is she aware of Bett's absurdity
in buzzing the King's 'Revenge', and does she
                            wonder,
if the plane's quite high enough to safely
loop just as the engine starts to pink?
Or is she too scared to speak, too scared to think?

Misogyny

'I had to ask him to stop; my head
felt as though it would come off.'
        Betty Behenna Daily Express 18/7/1938

Two girls who'd never flown before
subject to twists and rolls and loops
imprisoned in their cockpits while
a novice put the Hawk through hoops.

A reckless kid's high spirits mixed
with devilment in turns and twirls,
a joyride with so little joy
suggests that Edmund hated girls.

Flight

Tipping up the sun,
the sea, the sand and sky;
Edmund's showing off
his aerobatic skills,
ignoring the trainer's limits,
thrashing the Miles Hawk
as far she will go.

This is the joy of Edmund's life,
risk where he sees risk
as what it takes to be a knight of the air,
obviously immortal at nineteen
with all the ripping fun
of making young girls scream.

But braggadocio now brings death
to sunny Sunday evening Kent;
five thousand deckchairs creak
as holidaymakers rise to watch
a spinning flash of blue and silent splash.

Aerobatics

Would Marjorie have understood
the progress of the Hawk from stunting
to a sudden, unexpected stall?

Maybe after loops and rolls
a gentle drift towards the sea
might have seemed less frightening?

Until the waves rushed up and crashed
through Marjie's cockpit: icy water,
Edmund's cry, a slow darkness,

and death comes not from a fractured skull,
but a dreamy asphyxiation: the girl
on stage again at the Hippodrome.

Hippodrome

Margate Hippodrome,
a final cymbal crash
rouses a full house
to applaud the pretty girl
who dances for nothing
but gives her everything
these are the moments
when Marjorie feels alive.

Marjorie alive
in the sea for moments
she who was everything
and now is nothing
but an absent girl
from an empty house
where news comes of the crash
from a hapless aerodrome.

Joyride

Five thousand Sunday holidaymakers
in deckchairs and knotted handkerchiefs
watch Marjorie die in the sea off Margate.

A bigger crowd than ever came
to see her dance at the Hippodrome.

National fame at sixteen and a half—
tomorrow she'll plaster their Daily Mirrors:

'Boy pilot and beauty queen finalist die …'
Wrong boy, wrong plane, wrong joy, wrong fame.

Thrilling

'I would never have given her permission
to fly.'
             Florence Walk, Daily Mirror 18/7/1938

Bygone times when mothers might
forbid their working daughters, tell them
how to live their lives, advice
on how to be with boys, and why
to turn down flips in aeroplanes.

All this Marjorie must have known
but still she leapt at the thrill of a flight.

Mum surely would have understood,
upset at first then keen to hear
how Marjie circled round the dreadnaught,
looped and barrel-rolled and showed
the gaping watchers on the beaches
how it feels to be alive.

H.M.S. "REVENGE." DISPLACEMENT 25,750 TONS

Luck Of The Navy

His Majesty's Ship Revenge off Margate, sets
white-suited sailors free to hit the town's

arcades and cinemas and pubs; amazing
what there is to buy with five half-crowns.

And do they really walk with swaggered strut
the way they're shown in films, a bow-legged gait

as if on icy decks in force nine gales,
with cheery shanty piped from mate to mate?

Lock up your daughters, Margate battens down,
luck of the Navy, lucky for a few . . .

When mum warns Marj to stay away from tars,
she might have added novice pilots too.

Coral Belle

Hardy fuchsia, 'Coral Belle',
attractive plant that names the house
where Marjie and her parents live.

Hardy plant, whose hanging bells
can never ring as door-chimes ring
at 'Coral Belle' when policemen call.

'Boy Pilot And Girl Beauty Finalist Die As Plane Hits Sea'

Daily Mirror, 18/7/1938

A paragon of headline art:
eleven words that banner two
young deaths with brevity and truth.
What more can there be left to say?

So let's move on to other news:
Germany and the Czechs, a rumour denied,
a missing man is sought for murder,
the King to leave for France tomorrow.

Franco advance, Republican retreat,
two Arabs killed in Palestine,
Farnes is back in England's Test Team,
Roosevelt to visit Canada.

Queen Mary of Rumania,
whose state of health is far from good
will rest at Pelesh Palace (where
she'll die at half-past five this evening).

Jap raid on China, Canton bombed,
Detectives sleep in nursing home,
Drink Ovaltine and note the Difference!
Likely return of rain today.

Summer Night

At the end of another lovely day spent walking,
sunbathing and playing tennis, they watch
the sun set perfectly behind the pier.

And as the last bar and café closes
Margate holidaymakers — Did
you see the plane crash? — make their
sleepy way to hotel rooms and boarding
houses for a nightcap or mug of Ovaltine.

Then over the town the lights begin
to wink as Margate falls asleep.

A mile or so beyond the pier,
the waves, still restless, lift up from
their blackness, a girl's white arm.

God Loves Best

Loves more than broken Vic and Flo,
love for an only daughter dead
as great as love on earth can go.

Her dancing shoes and empty bed
remind them what is lost and gone,
with endless grief, their lives undone.

Yes, God loves best and takes their daughter,
soothes the heart when pain is raw,
imagine not her death by water

but Marj at peace for evermore.
Loss of their only child God's grant,
a gift that anyone might want.

Lost Hero

As one of Winston's plucky Few,
Edmund would have slotted in,
bantered lingo round the mess,
flown his Spit or Hurrie madly

as he'd flown the Hawk at Margate,
skill and nerve sky high as Heinkel
kills would swastika his kite,
a hero correctly set in time.

Two years too soon he whirled and dived
above the Channel, but only to frighten
Marjorie, not Nazis, leaving
the Few to save us by themselves.

Heartfelt Appeal

With Edmund dead, pulled from the wreck,
the broken Hawk lost to the sea —
no one thought to leave a buoy
to show where Marjorie might be.

And everyone who could have found her,
Council, Police, the dreadnought's crew
with teams of expert divers, all,
it seems, had something else to do.

The local rag set up a fund,
appealed for residents to comb
their wallets, purses, pay a diver,
find the wreck, bring Marjie home.

And contributions soon came in:
a florin, sixpence — all some had —
Gazette gave two pounds, and a tenner
came from Edmund Betts's dad.

Two weeks. At last enough to fund
a diver for a day to feel
his way around the wreck — but then
a floating girl is found off Deal.

Finalist

Just four days after the aircraft's crash,
Marjorie was booked to be seen
by carnival judges elected to choose
    Margate's Carnival Queen.

Was Marjorie Walk so beautiful?
It's difficult to tell from snaps
the Monday papers' printed, Deanna
    Durbin clone perhaps?

She could have won — instead they chose
another girl with eye-appeal
who'd wave and smile as Marjorie
    bobbed in the sea off Deal.

Mayoral Kisses

'The Mayoress was a smiling onlooker
when the Mayor of Margate kissed the
Carnival Queen and her four Maids of
Honour after the 'coronation' at Margate
Winter Gardens last Thursday night.'

Thanet Gazette, 29/7/1938

Marjie, were you there
when the portly Mayor

of Margate, puffed and keen,
kissed the Carnival Queen —

and Maids of Honour too —
when it should have been you?

Carnival

Endless parade of smiles and waves,
milk floats proud as battleships,
cheesecake Wendy, Indian braves,
lost boys, Peter Pan with generous hips,
Hook's pirates, Nana; all willing slaves

to Carnival. And there's the Queen,
bride-white against the blue of sea,
as Maids of Honour primp and preen
the royal gown (hired for free
from Mrs Jarman) which should have been

for Marjorie. Do Vic and Flo
stare at the floats, or do they sit
at Coral Belle, forgo the show,
too fresh, too new this family split,
the weight of loss too soon to know.

At Jarman's Ladies Outfitters

That awful week at Jarman's when
old customers from Hythe or Herne
would sweep in through those ornate doors
    and ask for Marjorie.

'I'm sorry to have to tell you but ...'
'Young Marjorie up in a plane?
What could she have been thinking of?'
    It would be nice to know.

A shake of head, a shrug of shoulders,
they ask for someone else to serve them,
Marjie pushed to the back of the day,
    their question stays unanswered.

Why had she placed her life in the hands
of Edmund Leonard George Betts?
Was it his chat and confidence
    that made her feel grown-up?

Or was it the drudgery, six-days-a-week,
of serving snooty customers
who treated girls like scullery maids
    that made her want to fly?

Epithalamium

A wedding at sea, a half a mile off Margate,
the nuptials of Edmund Betts and Marjorie Walk,
　　two young people joined in marriage forever.

Five thousand favoured guests on Margate sands
witness the ceremony; winds light, sea calm,
　　a perfect summer evening for a wedding.

They married far too young and should have
waited,
seen the issue of his wayward heart:
　　two Margate graves a hundred yards apart.

Not Coping

It was the shame of losing you,
the thought we could have done much more
to keep you here. The guilt that grew
    inside our hearts, that door

too great to move, when all the while
you seemed so close, just out of reach —
our beauty queen on Margate beach,
    like Kodachrome: your smile.

Everything

'I did everything to make her happy.'
          Victor Walk, Daily Mirror 18/7/1938

Shamed because he wasn't there to save her,
to come between his daughter and that boy,
tell him what to do with his blasted plane,
take Marjie home to mum and Sunday tea.

He did everything to make her happy,
bought her clothes and rings and dancing lessons,
said how talented she was and how
every day she looked more beautiful.

But she was growing fast and leaving him
to read the Sunday papers on his own —
blue aeroplanes, boy pilots, sea and sky
took Marjorie away, too far, too high.

Two Faces Of Marjorie

Pictured the day after the crash:
Daily Mirror, front page lead,
a serious face which tells us nothing
of what Marjorie was like —
just a girl from 1938.

Thanet Gazette, the following Friday:
Marjorie snapped in the middle of a laugh
which strikes somehow a false note,
unflattering, inappropriate,
a joke frozen by sudden death.

Two photographs of Marjorie,
in each she wears the same dark dress;
two poses snapped on different days?
Two looks: comedy/tragedy masks,
a January girl who looks both ways.

Filling In The Blanks

Favourite Movie Actor   ....

Favourite Movie Actress   ....

Favourite Movie of 1937   ....

Favourite Dance Band   ....

Favourite Male Vocalist   ....

Favourite Female Vocalist ....

Favourite Radio Comedian ....

Favourite Radio Programme.....................

Favourite Weekly Magazine.....................

Could we know Marjie by those she liked,
what popular stars she loved the best,
what make-up, magazines she bought,
what shoes she wore, how she was dressed?

But fashions change, girls can't ignore,
the latest trends and switch together;
unless they die young, then they're stuck
with Shearer, March, Film Fun forever.

Floating

Floating in the sea, not beautifully, artistically
like Millais' Ophelia, but jumbled, random,
blown up by body gas, still smart in leather
flying helmet but block holes for eyes,
summer dress rucked up to red blotched bitten
thighs — two weeks she's drifted with
the wind and tide, a beauty queen attractive
only to the gape of fish and bill of seabird.

Three miles off Deal she's found by pleasure boat,
a prize strange and repellent; let's not ask
Vic or Flo to claim this as their daughter;
let them hold the damp print dress, the ring,
the pretty pendant broach, which say that once
these things were part of Marjorie Cynthia Walk.

Putrefaction

That rotting, bloated, stinking thing
pulled from the sea three miles off Deal
would win no beauty contest, bring
no garlands home to Coral Belle,
bewitch no gaze with eye-appeal.

Two weeks in summer waters show
how time can change a lively teen
who can't be shown to Vic or Flo
but must be coffined out of sight,
a beauty queen to reign unseen.

Marjorie's Puppet Dance

Her jerky arms as if on strings,
that pretty head without a thought,
two clapping hands which never meet,
a soppy stare precisely caught.

Until the gramophone runs down
and Marjie's legs sag at the knee,
a final flop like strings are cut,
a lifeless puppet all at sea.

Marjorie Dancing And Singing - 2

And so she danced and so she sang
until the floor and ceiling rang,
her act straight from the Hippodrome

where crowds had stood to stamp and cheer,
so different from the people here,
a show for folks in an old folks' home.

Blank stare, dead eyes, what can this mean?
jazz songs from shows they've never seen,
crisp taps from films they'll never see,

the entertainment world's moved on
since turns like Harry Champion,
this modern stuff's a mystery.

But Marjorie's a star and knows
that she must give it all in shows,
it's show business, part of the game!

And when they hear of Marjie's end,
one frowns and turns towards a friend,
'Wasn't she the girl who came ... '

First Funeral

As Marjorie floats with wind and tide,
the funeral of Edmund Betts
takes place at Holy Trinity.

A large turnout for a popular boy
with hymns and prayers and many friends
to say how wonderful he was.

Though no one says if he'd not been
locked safely in his coffin he'd
be safely locked in Maidstone gaol.

Three cars pass through the cemetery gate
crammed full with farewell cards and wreaths,
with one from Victor and Florence Walk.

INTO THE SUNSHINE OF GOD'S LOVE
"ELGY"
EDMUND LEONARD GEORGE BETTS,
OF ROCHESTER, KENT,
AGED 19 YEARS.
WHO LOST HIS LIFE WHEN HIS AEROPLANE
CRASHED INTO THE SEA ON JULY 17TH 1938.

"WE PARTED HERE IN THE HASTE OF THOSE
WHO WERE TOO BUSY TO CALL HIM FRIEND,
IT SEEMED A LIKE A PLEASANT ROAD
UNTIL THEIR WORLD ITSELF WOULD END."

47

INTO THE SUNSHINE OF GOD'S LOVE
"ELGY,"
EDMUND LEONARD GEORGE BETTS
OF ROCHESTER, KENT.
AGED 19 YEARS
WHO LOST HIS LIFE WHEN HIS AEROPLANE
CRASHED INTO THE SEA ON JULY 17th 1938

"HIS NAME LIVETH IN THE HEARTS OF THOSE
WHO HAVE BEEN BLEST TO CALL HIM FRIEND,
TO BLOSSOM LIKE A FRAGRANT ROSE,
UNTIL THEIR WORLD ITSELF SHALL END."

Marble Aeroplane

The surprise on seeing Edmund's tomb
is not the pure white aeroplane
atop a mass of blood-red granite,
though this is certainly odd enough,
but that the plane is not a generic
model but a perfect copy
of the Hawk in which he died.

The trouble taken to reproduce
the cockpits, engine, tail-plane, trousered
undercarriage, the shapely wings
with markings, all in pristine marble
surely would have delighted its pilot.
Engendered only indifference
from a grave a hundred yards away.

Duplicitous Stone

'... who lost his life when his aeroplane
        crashed into the sea...'

As if his Miles Hawk had flown
into the water by itself.

You can't expect his stricken parents
to blame their son for Marjie's death.

Too much sorrow to contemplate,
why should they bear this extra grief?

Better for everyone to believe
this Hawk had a mind of its own.

Broken Wing

Above the grave white marble wings,
one broken, the other stubbornly clings
to its rock-like stone of scarlet granite —
that holy metaphor again.

Like Charles Lindberg's little 'Spirit':
steel and timber raised above
to sanctify a pilot's love,
an angel as an aeroplane.

Empty Space

Observe the plane, Betts' name,
the superscription, then
a mass of empty space.

Room for other Betts'
to be recorded below,
but none of them came here.

Too far from Rochester,
uniqueness of the stone,
the grave too aeroplaney?

The Sunshine Of God's Love

'HIS NAME LIVETH IN THE HEARTS OF THOSE
WHO HAVE BEEN BLESSED TO CALL HIM FRIEND,
TO BLOSSOM LIKE A FRAGRANT ROSE,
UNTIL THEIR WORLD ITSELF SHALL END'.

Edmund Betts has been forgotten,
family, friends forgotten too.

The grave untended — how many years —
who last came here to think of him?

Someone comes with Tesco roses,
scrapes dead seasons from the urn,

and thinks about an unwise knight
who took a queen up for a flight.

The Lily And The Lamp

Victor and Florence leaf through pattern-books
of headstone prints as the mason waits to see
what sort of stone they'd like. He notes their looks
of pleasure here, of distaste there; the key

he tells them is to feel comfortable
with a gravestone they'll never grow tired of,
a form that has meaning with a special symbol
suited to a headstone for the one they love.

But what to make of the myriad angels, pitch
black granite slabs and Celtic crosses, that strike
the pair as being far too grand. Which
one to select? Now, what would Marjorie like?

At last they circle round the 'Resting' print
of genre lily and lamp with flame in white —

the lily for innocence, the lamp a glint
of immortality. Or endless night.

Florence Lilian Walk

A stricken mum beside the grave
clutching hold of Victor's sleeve;
among the mourners, some were shocked
at how like Marjorie she looked.

This spectre of the girl who died
is only fleeting, quickly laid;
relief the girl stays underground,
sleeps in her coffin safe and sound.

Dancing Master

Who taught Marjorie to dance?
A local dance school: beginners to advanced,
a favourite instructor who stepped
to view the open grave and wept,
one skilled in modern dance steps who
taught Marjie everything she knew?

Those skills so difficult to master
call for stamina from the dancer
until their muscles learn the moves,
the spinning waist, the clack of shoes,
when blood and sweat become worthwhile,
and all she has to do is smile.

Lost Among The Farewells

A final hopeless glance at the grave,
then Victor and Florence leave Marjorie
to the browning leaves of August.

The thought of her in the sea all that time,
until she was pulled aboard a boat,
then being forbidden to look at her,
they thought that was worst time.

But this is the worst time.

Marjorie's Inscription

Some letters fixed with metal pins
have come adrift, been lost, but leave
white shadows where the lettering
preserved the stone from weathering
and just about can still be read.

The grammar lets it down of course,
a simple slip a clerk or mason
might have fixed before the stone
was carted to the grave. Now only
pedants crave to see it changed.

Idée fixe, a father's grief
that had to tell how Marjorie died,
calamity too great to leave
with simple name and age and date —
the stone stands as an accusation.

A hundred yards away a greater
stone, more florid, topped with marble
aeroplane, whose letters chime
with perfect grammar, is in denial —
pretends the crash was accidental.

Loved By All?

A parents' excusable vanity,
like their insistence that Marjorie was happy?

With no one now alive to say,
you wouldn't know if she was loved at all.

Eighty years have seen the end
of love and anyone who loved the girl.

But there's a line in the Thanet Gazette —
'Five hundred filed past her open grave'.

Her Happy Life

Why would her parents want this known?
To tell the world what they'd lost in the crash,
to indite Edmund's iniquity,
to salve their loss and guilt in stone?

Was Marjorie happy, did misery
absent itself, were tears unknown,
her joy infectious, winning, brash,
can we believe these words in stone?

Brief happy life lived at a dash,
was this the soul of Marjorie?
Now none can tell, her days unknown,
with only words to speak in stone.

16½

That pathetic half—half now dropped away;
infantilising Marjorie,
the need to tell the readers of her stone
how a crash stole the life of their child.

Who knows if anyone else
shared her parents' view?
Was Marjorie so immature?
She held a job down, danced
and entertained for charity.

Or was her Janus birth date all too real,
too young to live in a world of careless men,
16½ and still a child. Then.

Lost Life

To lose a life as if someday
        it might again be found,
life unforfeited, back one day,
        existence like a round.

Marjie's stone, a simple signpost,
        points the way she went,
when eighty years ago a new ghost
        twirled round graves in Kent.

Happy in life, no sighs or groans,
        her laughter everywhere,
she's moving still through trees and stones,
        light feet that dance on air.

Prankster

'In December, 1937, Betts was fined £5 at Margate
Police Court for flying low over his old school.'
                              Thanet Gazette 18/8/1938

'An Air Ministry telegram warning pilots against
the danger of stunting in the Miles Hawk was
brought to Betts' notice on the afternoon of
Sunday, June 19th, 1938.'
                              Coroner's Inquest, 13/8/1938

'I knew Eddie Betts very well and he was a likable
chap, although a little inclined to show off.'
        Gladys Batchelor, Aviatrix, Bygone Kent 1/6/1983

It was too much to ask a boy,
who saw the world from aeroplanes,
that he should look inside himself.

What would he find beneath the shell
of confidence, the carapace
where ego and self-interest lie?

At nineteen, boys do not perceive
themselves as others see them; pranksters
think they entertain the world,

and showing off is merely showing
everyone how good you are,
it's Betts' idea of being honest.

Ego, confidence, the grin
of perfect certainty. Of course
the girl is safe to fly with me!

Prangster

Missing everything but the sea
Amateurishly over-confident
Right rudder or left? Betts' mind goes blank
Jerks the stick back into his midriff
Only there's not enough height
Really not enough skill or experience
If he had another thousand feet to play with
Everything would be tickety-boo.

Waiting for the inevitable crash in
A frozen-frame moment he sees his pilot pals
Laughing their heads off at him for pranging the
Kite (forgetting all about the girl).

Two Birds Of A Feather

Squadron Leader Charles Edward Eckesley-
Maslin, Manager of Ramsgate Airport,
tells the coroner that Edmund Betts was
perfectly capable of flying stunts,
goes on to also claim, the Miles Hawk
a suitable plane for aerobatic flight.

Two lies which Eckesley-Maslin knows are lies,
but then the man, like Edmund, is a dasher,
a hothead who thumbs his nose at authority,
a life lived taking chances, he sees no reason
to further grieve the boy's poor parents by telling
the Court that Edmund's ego killed the girl.

Beyond The Realms Of Possibility

'It was not beyond the realms of possibility
that the passenger, Miss Walk, caught her feet
in the rudder bar and caused the accident.'

Coroner's summing up at the inquest, 13/8/1938

Those dancers legs that might
have kicked the bar, upset
the character of flight,

the Miles Hawk too low
to regain lift, green walls
of water crash, engulf...

The Coroner presumes:
what made him think the girl
might be responsible?

For only God would know
if Marjie crashed the plane
because she had long legs.

Like Rashomon

'My attention was drawn to the aeroplane by my little boy.
At that time it was only about twenty feet in the air and
about to nose dive into the water. It came down with a
roar and hit the water with a tremendous crash.'
Frederick Cross

'The machine circled round the Revenge and afterwards,
when it was between the shore and the battleship, it
looped the loop. I expected it to continue looping when it
spun two or three times and dived straight into the sea.'
Mrs Norman

'The last loop it completed was very low, and after that the
plane made off in the direction of Foreness Point for a dis-
tance of about 300 yards. Then the engine seemed to cut
out and it dropped like a stone without a sound into the
water. I was only about 400 yards away and did not hear
any roar of the engine.'
George Popple

Three versions picture death, like 'Rashomon',
a clear bright day, three witnesses well placed
to see the accident, yet all saw something

different. They testified before
the Coroner, but what was he to make
of their conflicting evidence? No one

was called before the court to say if there was
anything mechanically wrong with the Hawk,

the plane was lost and never would be found.

A thousand seamen aboard the Revenge trained
to have sharp eyes apparently saw nothing;
not one of the crew was called before the court.

Five thousand holidaymakers on Margate sands
saw nothing, with no one summoned from factories
and offices to give their evidence.

The Coroner declared the crash a simple
accident and did not blame the boy,
or girl — let's close the book and bury the bodies.

Chorine Or Star?

A chorine in a seaside show
with whisky comic pinching bums,
is this the Marjorie we know,
all arms and legs, all teeth and gums,
a sequined second-rate junior pro?

If she had talent would she wait
for opportunities to crack
the London shows and grab a date
with Loss or Ambrose, Roy or Jack,
Café Royale, eight till late?

Too young to tell what play or part
she might have won if fate had flipped
her life and given her a start,
if she'd been fortunate and skipped
the silly flight that stopped her heart.

October

The empty chair by the radiogram
where Marjorie would twiddle the dial
until a dance band filled the room.

Then she would tap her hands and feet
and move her head from side to side
and light her face with a special smile.

Remembering. But seeing her sudden
immaculate face brings tears
without the balm of consolation.

Marjorie's Things

Time at last to clear her bedroom,
skirts and blouses, spangled dresses,
dancing shoes and evening gloves,

her movie annuals, Photoplays,
green gramophone and Lew Stone discs,
the League of Friends will take them all.

Her trophies, badges, school reports
and birthday cards, her mother keeps.
Florence collects the underwear

then watches whirls of smoke rise through
bare winter trees into a Margate
sky that let her daughter down.

First Christmas

A vast amount of snow fell in Kent
on Christmas Day in 1938,
so unexpectedly that trains and busses
    stopped, no taxis could be had.

Did Vic and Florence trudge past All Saints Church
to Margate cemetery, to stand beside
a snowy stone and dream of July days
    before the boy and aeroplane?

17 July, 1948

It will be the same this year as last year,
this month as last month, every Sunday,
the slow walk to the cemetery
with flowers for a daughter's grave.

A quarter hour of staring at
her stone and thinking of her face,
and wondering if she's looking at them,
or if she's with God, who loves her best.

IN LOVING MEMORY OF
OUR DAUGHTER
MARJORIE CYNTHIA WALK
AGED 16 YEARS
WHOSE HAPPY LIFE ENDED BY
AN AIR-CRASH JULY 12TH 1938.
LOVED BY ALL
BUT GOD LOVES BEST
SO WITH HIM OUR LOVED ONE RESTS
ALSO HER DEAREST FATHER
VICTOR FRANKLIN WALK
DIED JAN. 4TH 1951.
AGED 57 YEARS
"UNITED IN GOD'S KEEPING."
AND FLORENCE LILIAN WALK
BELOVED WIFE OF THE ABOVE
WHO PASSED AWAY 2ND MARCH 1955.
AGED 58 YEARS

IN LOVING MEMORY OF
OUR DAUGHTER
MARJORIE CYNTHIA WALK
AGED 16½ YEARS
WHOSE HAPPY LIFE ENDED BY
AN AIR-CRASH JULY 17TH 1938.
LOVED BY ALL
BUT GOD LOVES BEST
SO WITH HIM OUR LOVED ONE RESTS
ALSO HER DEAREST FATHER
VICTOR FRANKLIN WALK
DIED JAN 4TH 1951
AGED 57 YEARS
"UNITED IN GOD'S KEEPING"
AND FLORENCE LILIAN WALK
BELOVED WIFE OF THE ABOVE
WHO PASSED AWAY 2ND MARCH 1956
AGED 58 YEARS

United In God's Keeping

In less than twenty years the Walks are gone,
    both parents interred with Marjorie,
    their names and ages inscribed upon
her stone inside the marble space left free.

A wish that they should always be together —
    all too soon granted — what hopeless pain
    is ended here; three lives that never
should have crossed a boy and aeroplane.

Coffin House

'Gwendolin House', a pleasant name,
but known to locals as 'Coffin House',
because of its shape, and also its close
proximity to Margate cemetery.

Here, in the summer of 1938,
two cortèges drove on their way
to the cemetery gates. But not together.
Two teenagers died together but were buried
in July and August of that year.

Then hardly any traffic would have slowed
their processions. Now, with traffic lights
and 'Gwendolin House' demolished to ease
the flow of vehicles, it's a bottleneck
best dodged, unless in hot summer cars
you like to stare through cemetery gates.

What Can The Living Do For The Dead

but stare at gravestones,
count the years from date of death,
consider the age
and state of the stone? The choice
of porous marble
over metallic granite
seen to be unwise, the former
weathering,
making names and dates unclear,
blotches of lichen greying letters and numbers
degrading the stone into
illegibility —
a bore to read.
Why read this one?
What can the living do for the dead
but read their gravestones?

Wrapt In Sleep

Wrapt in sleep, a winding sheet
about Miss Marjorie Cynthia Walk,
white and cool in Kentish chalk,
deep and deathless, prim and neat.

Dreamless dark, no clock to keep
this girl awake, no shrill alarms,
but safe within redemption's arms,
assured and spellbound, rapt in sleep.

BOOKS BY THIS AUTHOR

Man In The Long Grass, Iron Press

If you have enjoyed this book, please consider leaving a review on Amazon. I would also be most grateful to receive notice of any errors, typos etc. at hollylps@yahoo.com

Cover picture: Botany Bay, Margate, close to where the Miles Hawk crashed.

Printed in Poland
by Amazon Fulfillment
Poland Sp. z o.o., Wrocław

56858448R00047